The MOMS' Book

FOR THE MOM WHO'S Best AT Everything

The MOMS' Book

FOR THE MOM WHO'S

Best AT Everything

BY ALISON MALONEY

SCHOLASTIC INC.
New York   Toronto   London   Auckland   Sydney
Mexico City   New Delhi   Hong Kong   Buenos Aires

To my mom,
the best in the world

Library of Congress Cataloging-in-Publication data is available.

ISBN-13: 978-0-545-04211-6
ISBN-10: 0-545-04211-9

First published in Great Britain in 2007 by Michael O'Mara Books Limited.

Text copyright © 2007 by Michael O'Mara Books Limited
Illustrations copyright © 2007 by Michael O'Mara Books Limited
Cover design by Angie Allison
Cover illustration by Getty Images

Illustrations on pages 11–14, 16 (bottom), 17, 20–22, 27, 57, 61, 80, 81 © 2007 by David Woodroffe; page 33 © Getty Images; pages 1, 2, 5, 7, 10, 49, 58, 61 (bottom), 66, 72, 74, 89, 90, 91, 92, 93, 94 (top), 95, 96, 99, 102, 115, 117 © Images courtesy of retroclipart.com.

12 11 10 9 8 7 6 5 4 3 2   8 9 10 11 12 13/0

Printed in the U.S.A.
First American edition, April 2008

Contents

CONTENTS

Introduction

Nobody knows how to do everything quite as well as a mom does. From nursing scraped knees to mending broken hearts, it's Mom who has a practical solution for every crisis while always keeping her head.

Who else could spend all day working, cleaning, and shopping and *still* show up on time after school, with a smile and a welcoming hug, wearing the hottest new fashion? Who else can juggle career commitments while fulfilling the demands of a busy home life and *still* have time to organize playdates and birthday parties?

Nothing fazes the mom who's best at everything. If there are six more kids than expected for dinner, she'll whip up a wonderful meal in minutes. If the children have left a mess all over the stairs, she'll do a "quick" steam-clean without smudging her

makeup or getting a hair out of place. And she *never* loses her temper. Her house is always cozy and welcoming, and when the children come home from school, they are fed healthy, nutritious snacks that they actually like!

But, perfect as you are, every mom occasionally needs a helping hand. Here you can learn how to throw the perfect party, spend fun-packed afternoons with your kids, and, best of all, make the most of your child-free time.

Share some stories about great moms, pushy moms, and downright awful moms, and celebrate the multifaceted existence that we call motherhood.

Finally, just remember that to your own kids, you will always be *the mom who's best at everything.*

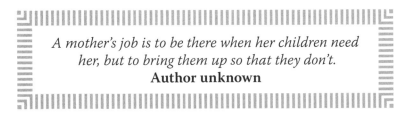

A mother's job is to be there when her children need her, but to bring them up so that they don't.
Author unknown

The Wakeup Call

Before the kids are old enough to go to school, you do everything in your power to make them stay in bed as long as possible in the morning. Remember those weekends when the kids would jump out of bed at six a.m. and drag you downstairs to make breakfast?

But as soon as they go to school, it all stops! Now try to get them up at seven in the morning, and they pull the covers over their heads and groan. No matter what you do, they refuse to budge, turning the morning into a huge last-minute rush and making everybody late for school.

To help you avoid the morning chaos, here are the ten best ways to get your kids out of bed.

1. Put your favorite Barry Manilow album in their CD player and turn the volume up full blast.

2. Threaten to dock their allowance for every extra minute they don't budge.

3. Put a wet washcloth down the back of their pajama top.

4 Tell them their favorite program is on TV — whether it's true or not.

5 Tickle their feet.

6 Go out the front door and slam it loudly so they think you are leaving without them. (This only works with younger children. Teenagers breathe a sigh of relief and go back to sleep.)

7 Tell them there is only one bowl of their favorite cereal left and that their little brother is about to eat it.

8 Start picking up toys, computer games, and favorite clothes from their floor and closet and putting them in a garbage bag.

9 Tell them their least favorite relative is about to visit — they'll be dressed and out the door in ten seconds flat!

10 Scream and point at the bottom of their bed. Then, without any explanation, run out of the room. (Obviously this tactic only works occasionally, so it is best to use it only as a last resort.)

Lights-Out

Of course, the evening brings the opposite problem. You're exhausted but the kids are all wound up. They want to finish their video game or watch the end of a movie and there's always something they just *have* to do before bedtime.

If bedtime is a tug-of-war, here are the ten best ways of winning that battle and getting the children to bed.

1. Keep them away from cookies, candy, and soda — or they'll be bouncing on the bed rather than sleeping in it!

2. Use your thespian skills and read them a bedtime story — but don't make it *too* exciting.

3. Make them run around the backyard for several hours when they get home from school. That way, they'll be so tired that they'll crawl into bed early.

4. Milk and bananas are both supposed to aid sleep, so whip up a banana smoothie — and don't add sugar!

5. Lavender is great for making kids sleepy. Just add a drop of lavender oil to their evening bath.

6. Turn off the TV. There may be tantrums, but if you stand firm, this usually has them traipsing upstairs on time. This doesn't work, however, if they have a TV in their room.

⑦ Alter the minute hand on the clock so that they think it's half an hour later than it really is! This works especially well in the winter when it gets dark earlier.

⑧ As with the wakeup call, the threat of a pesky relative dropping by should get them into bed in no time.

⑨ If they have a CD player in their room try soothing music or an audiobook that will help lull them to sleep.

⑩ If all else fails, let them stay up as late as they want. Hopefully, they'll learn their lesson when they have to spend the next day sleep-deprived in school.

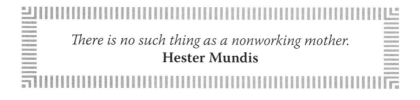

There is no such thing as a nonworking mother.
Hester Mundis

Curing the Heebie-jeebies

You've just tucked your little one in when a wail that would frighten a banshee rings out. Chances are your child is not being attacked by an ax-wielding maniac, but is simply having a bad dream.

Try the following tips to soothe away your child's frightening nightmares.

1. Make a hot, milky drink for your traumatized son or daughter. These usually work nicely to calm the nerves.

2. Tell your child a pleasant story — but make sure it doesn't contain witches, vampires, ghosts, or monsters!

3 Paint a relaxing scene in your child's head. For example, tell them to imagine they are on a beach with waves lapping against the shore, and that they are building sand castles with their friends. Sound effects can help if you are any good at lapping waves!

4 Put a song in their head. Think of their favorite song and see if they can remember the lyrics — silently, of course. This is not such a great idea if their musical tastes happen to extend to heavy metal or rap.

5 Talk about your next vacation or day trip. Reminding them of something they are looking forward to can take their mind off whatever is scaring them.

6 Stay with them for a while and stroke their hair or back to soothe them.

7 Encourage them to tell you what was in the dream that frightened them. Then suggest ways to overcome their fears. This can be done the following morning and may help prevent recurring nightmares.

8 Tell the children that whatever is in their dreams can't hurt them and that you are there to protect them. Let them know it is safe to go back to sleep.

9 Switch on a night-light if the dark is making them more afraid.

10 *Don't* take them into your own bed. This sends a subconscious message that their bed is frightening and yours is safe. You'll never get them to go back to their own bed again!

Party Time

Birthdays used to mean cake and ice cream at home, a game of Pin the Tail on the Donkey, and a few presents. But nowadays, kids want nothing less than a full-scale extravaganza such as an outing to the movie theater with twenty-five friends. It can get incredibly expensive, not to mention increasingly competitive, so how about getting back to the basics and entertaining the kids at home? If you can face the inevitable mess and cope with the occasional spillage, you can still throw the best party in the world — right in your very own living room!

The Theme's the Thing

All the best parties have themes. Whether it's pirates, fairies, or Harry Potter, make sure the theme is reflected in every part of the event, and not just the costumes. Below are just a few suggestions that are perennially popular with children.

Swashbuckling Pirates

Costumes: Pirate clothes are relatively simple to make and don't have to cost a fortune. All you need is a big, baggy shirt tied around the waist with a sash made out of a long winter scarf or a lengthy strip of plain material. Next, find an old pair of leather boots, and a baggy pair of pants, or an old pair made to look frayed around the knees and a striped T-shirt. Then tie a scarf around the head, add an eye patch and a toy sword, and you have your very own Captain Jack.

Decorations: Fill the house with Jolly Roger flags. If you're lucky, you might be able to find balloons with skulls and cross-bones but, if not, black and red ones work just as well. Treasure maps and chests filled with chocolate coins also make good decorations.

If you are having the party outside, build a pirate ship using wooden pallets as a raft. Then add broomsticks with old sheets as sails, a Jolly Roger flag, and a treasure chest. If you have any old jewelry around, add that for effect.

Food: Use cookie cutters to cut the sandwiches into interesting shapes. Hands (signifying the one that Captain Hook lost to a crocodile in *Peter Pan*), treasure chests, boats, and sails are all possibilities.

If you're new to baking, a simple cake with a skull and crossbones decoration will do. If you enjoy baking, a treasure chest cake is easy to make and can be filled with sweets or chocolate coins (p. 10), or you can make a pirate ship cake (p. 12). If you hate baking, see if your local bakery or supermarket has any pirate-themed cakes that you can purchase.

Activities: Have a treasure hunt in the house or, if the weather is nice, in the yard. Hide or bury a box or chest full of chocolate coins, and place clues all over the house to lead the children to it. Tip: You'll find it's a lot easier to start at the point where you've hidden the treasure and work backward when writing the clues.

Another fun activity is getting the children to decorate some cookies with pirate faces. Mix some icing with a little water so that it can be spread easily, then provide different types of candies to make the facial features.

Games: Play Pin the Tail on the Parrot. Draw or photocopy a large picture of a pirate with a parrot on his shoulder, or just the parrot itself. Then draw and cut out a tail and put a piece of double-sided tape on the back of it, and tape it to a wall at about the height of a child's head. Blindfold the children and ask them to pin the tail on the picture of the parrot. Kids find this hilarious!

Pirate-Themed Recipes

Treasure Chest Cake

Ingredients for the cake mixture:
9 tbsp butter
3 cups sugar
3 eggs, beaten
18 tbsp self-rising flour
4 tbsp cocoa powder
1 cup of water

Ingredients for icing:
3½ tbsp softened butter
8 tbsp confectioners' sugar
3 tbsp cocoa powder
¼ cup milk
silver/gold cake decorations

1. Grease an 8-inch square cake pan.

2. Mix the butter, sugar, eggs, flour, cocoa powder, and water in a large bowl with an electric mixer, or by hand, until the mixture is smooth.

3. Pour into the cake pan and bake for one and a half hours at 350°F. When baked, let stand for five minutes and then remove it from the pan and place on a wire rack.

4. When the cake has cooled, cut a 5-inch square from the center of the cake to about half the depth. (The kids will love eating this part!) Mix the icing, cocoa powder, butter, and milk, and then ice the remaining cake.

5. Create the illusion of metal studs with blobs of white icing or with silver or gold cake decorations. Then fill the center with gold coins and candy.

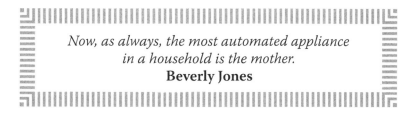

Now, as always, the most automated appliance in a household is the mother.
Beverly Jones

Pirate Ship Cake

2 baked 9-inch or 10-inch round cakes
(using the Treasure Chest Cake recipe)
4 cups chocolate butter icing (recipe on p. 10)
Rolos (in foil wrappers)
Whoppers
Kit Kat bars
straws and toothpicks
chocolate Twizzlers
paper sails (with skull and crossbones
either drawn on or printed from a computer)

1 Cut the cakes in half, to make semicircles. Stack each semicircle on top of one another, to create a half-barrel shape, and attach them more firmly by spreading a thin coat of chocolate icing in between each layer.

2 Slice off the bottom curve to make the ship sit better, then turn it upright, with the longer side on top.

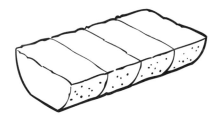

3 Chill the cake in the fridge, then cover with the chocolate icing, inserting a Kit Kat at one end of the ship to create a prow. Chill for another hour to firm the icing.

④ Place chocolate Twizzlers around the edge of the deck. Then add a pile of Whoppers for cannonballs and Rolos (still wrapped in their gold foil) for barrels. Stick the sails onto the toothpicks.

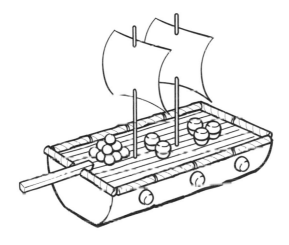

⑤ For the cannons, place three unwrapped Rolos on each side of the ship, held in place with toothpicks. The birthday candles can be placed on the deck.

Fantastical Fairies

Costumes: Think pink. Many young girls have pretty princess dresses these days, but otherwise a leotard and a simple tutu work just fine. Wings are inexpensive to buy, but should you want to make your own, you will need strong but pliable wire (like coat-hanger wire), some netting or old white tights, and some elastic.

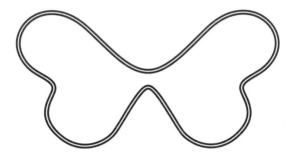

Bend the wire into the shape of butterfly wings and then stretch an old pair of tights over the frame. Tape any excess material to the underside. Once secure, you can now attach some sequins or use glitter paint on the wings to give them that extra sparkle. To make this essential accessory wearable, tie a piece of elastic around the center of the wings, making two loops to go over your child's shoulders like backpack straps.

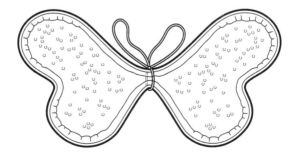

To make a wand, simply cut out a star from cardboard and paint it with glitter paint, or cover it in aluminum foil. Then attach it to the end of a long thin stick, or a pretty pencil.

Decorations: If you are having the party outside, decorate the garden with wind chimes and white Christmas lights. Give the kids bubble mixture, because bubbles flying around the yard will give it an enchanted look. Tie silver stars made out of cardboard and tin foil to the branches of the trees and add strings of beads, such as the ones used to decorate Christmas trees.

If you have a playhouse in your backyard, it can be transformed into a fairy grotto with colorful crepe paper and white Christmas lights. If it's a winter party, put the lights inside and decorate the walls with pink crepe paper and silver stars. Sprinkle the party table with tiny glittery stars or hearts.

Activities: Hide gold and silver chocolate coins and colorful candies around the house or yard, and give each child a "fairy cup." Then send them on a candy hunt! Encourage them by telling them they are "warm" when near a treasure and "cold" when far away.

Games: We've all played Musical Chairs, but with a lot of children it is difficult to manage this at home, so Musical Cushions is a great alternative for any party. Play it the same way as Musical Chairs but using cushions instead of chairs. This way, it's safer and easier!

Another exciting game is Pass the Parcel. To play, wrap a candy bar (or some other treat) in wrapping paper. Continue adding a layer of wrapping until you have about a dozen layers.

Now, sit the children in a circle and play part of a song as they pass the gift around. When the music stops, the person holding the gift gets to unwrap one layer. Continue until you have a winner.

Food: Bake some cookies in the shape of hearts and stars. Cupcakes are also a must (see p. 60), and if you want to make them into butterfly cupcakes, slice a 1-inch circle from the center and cut it in half making two semicircles, then add some butter icing and stick in the two semicircles so they come out the top and look like wings.

Peter Pan and Friends

This is a great party theme for both boys and girls because everyone can identify with the characters in this classic story.

Costumes: There are a variety of different costumes to choose from and most are easy to make. You can use the directions for pirates and fairies from before as templates for Smee, Captain Hook (with the addition of a plastic hook and a floppy hat), and Tinker Bell. Anyone going as Wendy really needs nothing more than a long nightgown. Tiger Lily will need a long brown tunic, cut with a fringe around the bottom, and decorated with a beaded belt. Long hair should be tied into two braids on either side of the face and decorated with thick, colorful hairbands, and a headdress can be made from a ring of cardboard, colored in a mosaic style, with a feather or two sticking straight up at the back.

Peter Pan's costume is probably the most difficult, but here is a simple way to make a great outfit.

You will need some green felt, fabric scissors, fabric glue, a red feather, a large green T-shirt (preferably old or inexpensive), some green tights, a belt, and a toy sword (or you can make your own).

1 Estimate the size of your child's head using a tape measure. Then draw a triangle on a piece of green felt, with the triangle base measuring the same as the circumference of your child's head, and the height equaling about half the length of the base.

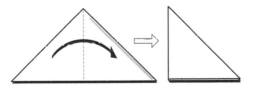

2 Cut out the triangle and fold it in half lengthwise. Glue the side edges together, leaving a tiny hole at the top.

3 Using a little glue, stick the feather into the hole.

④ Cut a jagged pattern along the bottom of the T-shirt and along the bottom of each sleeve.

⑤ Once your child has put on the customized T-shirt and the green tights, fasten the belt over the T-shirt, and add the fake sword (if you make it yourself, draw an outline of a sword on some cardboard — the sturdier the better — cut it out, and cover it with aluminum foil).

⑥ For the finishing touch, add the hat — making sure the glue is completely dry first, otherwise your Peter Pan may suffer premature hair loss!

Decorations: Turn the house or yard into Neverland. You could transform a playhouse into the Lost Boys' lair, or you could use pop-up tunnels and tents. If you have a small tent or a teepee, put that up for the Indian camp. A small wading pool filled with plastic balls makes a great lagoon. If the party is taking place inside, decorate the room with pirate flags and green crepe paper.

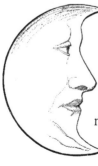

Mermaids' Lagoon can be created with strips of blue and green crepe paper mixed with strips of silver foil hanging down from walls or ceilings. Make a big moon, covered in foil, and cut out the shape of a pirate ship from black paper. Put the two together to make a simple, but very effective decoration. Don't forget the stars, especially the second star on the right!

Food: Make a pirate cake (p. 12), and bake cookies in the shape of Peter's hat, swords, and the moon and stars.

Activities: Hide treasure at Hangman's Cove where Captain Hook kept all his riches. Create a cavelike atmosphere in a large closet and hide a chest of gold coins there, then have a treasure hunt as described before.

Games: Play Hide from the Pirates. Outside, on the patio area or in the driveway, use chalk to draw circles, totaling one less than the number of kids present. Ask the children to move around in different ways (e.g. hop, run, walk, fly like Tinker Bell). Occasionally, you must call out "Hide from the pirates," which is the children's cue to scramble to find a "hole." The child who does not reach one in time has to stand in a "hole" for the rest of the game. The contest continues until the last one to get a "hole" wins the game.

Play Whose Shadow? In a darkened room with curtains closed, suspend a white sheet from the top of the door frame, making sure that the sheet reaches the floor. Split the kids into two teams, one on either side of the doorway. The team of kids in the room then take turns walking closely past the sheet, using a flashlight to cast their shadow on it. The other team then has to guess whose shadow is walking by each time. The team with the most correct guesses wins.

Fairy-tale Fun

This theme appeals particularly to girls, because many fairy-tale characters are princesses, but boys are certainly not excluded with so many princes and knights to choose from.

Costume: Any princess dress will do, although there are other alternatives. How about making a simple red cape for Little

Red Riding Hood (see below) or adapting a raggedy dress for Cinderella (the one she wore before she met Prince Charming)? Boys can go as knights by wearing a simple white tunic (a T-shirt with the sleeves cut off) with a shield or a cross drawn on it, and carrying a sword and shield. Glittery black tights make great chain mail (if you can persuade your little knight to wear them) and, you can make a cardboard crown and cover it with gold paint or silver foil.

To make Little Red Riding Hood's cape and hood:
You will need two pieces of red felt or fleece, the first measuring 80 by 40 inches and the second measuring 40 by 20 inches. (These are just estimates. It might be a good idea to do the measuring *before* buying the cloth to make sure you have enough.)

1. Measure from the back of your child's neck down to their knee to determine the length of the cape. Fold the longer piece of fabric in half and, using chalk or a pen, mark the length measurement down the crease, and also from left to right on the top edge of the fabric. Draw a curve between the two points to make a quarter-circle and cut along the curve to produce a semicircle. Cut out a rounded neckline in the middle of the semicircle.

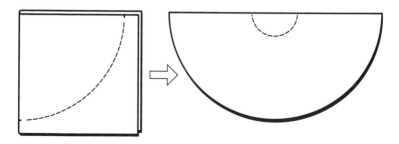

2 To make the hood you will need to cut out another semicircle. To judge its size, first measure from your child's eyebrows across the top of the head and down to the base of the neck. Add 3 inches and this will give you the radius of your semicircle. Fold

the fabric in half to make a square and, as above, mark the radius measurement down the crease, and also from left to right on the top edge of the fabric. Draw a curve between the two points to make a quarter-circle, and cut along it to produce a semicircle.

After you have cut out the hood shape, take note that it is the straight edge that will be framing the face. You need to gather up the curved edge and then sew it to the rounded neckline of the cape.

3 Cut the vertical slits just below the neckline of the main cape and thread a long red ribbon through, leaving plenty to use as a tie.

Decorations: Cover the house with sumptuous colors and fabrics. If you have any velvet, fake fur, or gold fabric, drape it over chairs to give them a royal look. If not, cover the chairs with red or purple crepe paper or gold wrapping paper. Hang a foil curtain at the door of the party room and create the feeling of a ball, with dim lighting and silver foil and crepe paper streamers. Make a throne for the birthday girl by putting a cushion on a dining-room chair and decorating the back with pink and purple strips.

Food: Make a princess cake — it's easier than it sounds! Use a 2-quart ovenproof Pyrex glass mixing bowl to bake a normal sponge cake (either from scratch — see Treasure Chest Cake recipe on page 10 — or from a mix if you want to save time). Leave the freshly baked cake to cool, then turn it upside down on a plate. Stick a Barbie-type doll (preferably with the top half clothed!) into the baked cake, so that the cake becomes her skirt. If need be, scoop a little bit of the cake out to make way for her legs — also a good excuse to be the first to taste it! Then decorate the skirt with icing and cake decorations however you wish.

There are plenty of princess-themed cookies and candies out there for the party food, but you could also try heart- and star-shaped sandwiches, royal strawberries (strawberries dipped in chocolate), and pink drinks (fruit punch or pink lemonade).

Activities: Let the children make their own crowns and princess hats. Cut out the shapes of crowns and the cone hats before the children arrive, and provide paint, glitter, and stick-on gems for them to use. Obviously this can be very messy! The boys can also make shields and swords using cardboard, paint, and aluminum foil. Alternatively, if it's a girl's party, buy an inexpensive bracelet-making kit, or just some beads and thin elastic, and let them make their own jewelry. This activity can keep kids happily occupied for hours and they also get to take their creation home at the end of the party.

Games: Princess and the Pea — *Part I.* Start this game by telling the story of the princess and the pea. Then, ask the girls to find their own "pea." Arrange four pillows in a row on the floor and place a small ball under one of them. Each girl must sit on the pillows in turn, and guess which one the ball is under. Move the ball every time, and if you want to make it even more difficult, use a marble.

Princess and the Pea — *Part II.* Fill a jar with split peas, counting them as you go. The children each guess how many peas they think are in the jar, and the winner gets a small prize.

The Queen Says . . . This game is simply the royal version of Simon Says.

Stick the Kiss on the Frog. This game is played just like Pin the Tail on the Donkey. Enlist the help of someone artistic

to draw a large frog on a sheet of posterboard and tape it to an easel or wall. Then draw and cut out several red lips using cardboard and write the names of the guests on them. Place a piece of tape on each pair of lips. Use a purple satin sash for the blindfold. Each child takes a turn trying to stick his/her set of lips onto the frog and the winner is the one who sticks his/hers closest to the frog's mouth.

Pajama Party

This type of party is perfect for older children who may be past the "dressing-up stage" but still love the excitement of a sleepover.

Costumes: Pajamas (nice and easy!)

Accessories: Tell everyone to bring his/her own sleeping bags and pillows, but make sure you borrow a couple of spares just in case.

Food: As a special treat, prepare a "midnight feast," although you don't have to wait until the middle of the night to serve it. Some of the best midnight snacks are pizza, ice cream sundaes, fresh fruit, popcorn, and pretzels.

Games: Telephone — a message is whispered into the ear of one child who then whispers it to the next child, and so on. Some of the resulting sentences can be hilarious. To start, you could cut out newspaper headlines and substitute real names with those of the guests. But keep the sentences silly, and avoid anything that might be true, insulting, or embarrassing.

Quick on the Draw is always a huge hit. Write down words, phrases, and names of books, films, etc. on slips of paper and put them in a large bowl. Then divide the children into two teams and give each a pad of paper and a pencil. One member of each team has two minutes to draw as many of the phrases as possible and his/her team must guess each one before moving on to the next. No words or numbers can be written down and the child who is drawing must not speak or gesture. The team with the most points wins.

Life is only lived full-time by women with children.
Marguerite Duras

Other Possible Party Themes

* The Wizard of Oz
* Harry Potter
* Disney characters
* The Wild West
* Superheroes
* The Circus

General Party Games for Younger Children

Switch!

Divide the children into two teams and take the first group into another room. Then get them to switch items of clothing, such as belts, shoes, sweaters, and socks, and come back into the room. The other team must guess who has changed which items of clothing. You will need to keep a note of who is wearing what so that you can keep track of the scores. Make sure there is the same number of switches for each turn, as the team who guesses the most is the winner. If the children are not wearing enough accessories or easily swappable clothing, get them to dress up first.

Puzzle Hunt

Take six different-colored pieces of paper and on each one, draw a person, such as a clown or a pirate, depending on the theme of the party. It could also be an animal like a frog, a dog, or a fish, as long as they can be cut into six identifiable pieces. Cut around the outline of your character and then cut into six pieces — for example, head, body, two legs, and two arms. Number them 1 to 6. Then, tape the thirty-six separate pieces around the house or backyard. Divide the  children into six teams and give them each a color to find. The first team to return with all six pieces of the puzzle, and to put the character together, is the winner.

Hot Potato

Ask the children to sit in a circle and give one child a balloon or ball. If there are lots of children, two balloons may be used. Put some music on. The children must pass the balloon around as quickly as they can. Whoever is holding it when the music stops is out. The last child left is the winner.

For Older Children

The Name Game

A similar game to Quick on the Draw, but for the less artistic. On separate scraps of paper, write down the names of as many famous people as you can, making sure they are people who the children will know, and then put the paper in a bowl. A mixture of fictional characters, such as Bart Simpson, and real celebrities, such as Brad Pitt, usually works well. Then one member of each team has two minutes to describe as many famous people as possible to his/her team members without mentioning the name on the paper or using a "sounds like" clue. Their team gets a point for each person the player names correctly, and after each team member has had his/her turn, the team with the most points is the winner.

Truth or Dare

Write questions for the children on slips of paper and put them in a bowl. They can be slightly personal, such as "Who is your boyfriend?" mixed with quiz questions such as "What's the capital of France?" or "What is 12 x 6?" In another bowl, place slips of paper with dares for refusing to answer a question, telling a lie, or getting it wrong. Make them fun, but not too embarrassing or scary. For example, "Hop on one leg while singing 'Twinkle Twinkle Little Star,'" or "Walk around the room like a gorilla."

Mystery Melodies

Before the party, record a few seconds of your child's favorite pop songs with thirty-second gaps between each. When all the children are there, play a few seconds at a time. The first child to guess the song (and the artist, if you want to make it harder) gets a point. If nobody guesses it the first time, add a little more of the song until someone does.

Heroic Moms

Most moms say they would do anything for their children, but rarely is this put to the test. Here we pay tribute to those mothers who went the extra mile out of love, bravery, or just plain instinct.

Eleanor of Aquitaine (c. 1122–1204)

Known as the "Grandmother of Europe," Eleanor of Aquitaine wielded political influence over the continent through her marriages, her children, and the marriages of her daughters.

At fifteen, the Duchess of Aquitaine was married to the French king Louis VII. She bore him two daughters and was highly influential in state matters during her reign. In 1147, she led a company of 300 women to the Crusades, alongside her husband and his army, to fight as well as tend to the wounded. However, after Louis became jealous about her relationship with an uncle, their marriage was annulled in 1152.

Six weeks later, swamped by suitors, Eleanor married Henry of Normandy, soon to become King Henry II of England. Together they had three daughters and five sons, which was no easy feat for a woman in her thirties in the twelfth century.

In 1173, Henry's sons Richard (later the Lionheart) and John (Lackland) rebelled against their father, and Eleanor took her children's side (as mothers are wont to do). Caught trying to flee the country, Eleanor was imprisoned for fifteen years and was only freed upon her husband's death in 1189. After her release, she granted amnesty to prisoners and ensured the loyalty of the English to her son Richard the Lionheart. When he was captured, she raised the ransom and secured his release.

The marriages of her daughters to rulers throughout Europe gained her further influence and, at the age of seventy, she made an epic journey across the Pyrenees to escort Berengaria of Navarre to Cyprus, where she married Richard.

Eleanor died at the grand old age of eighty, but was active up until the very end. Shortly before her death she successfully defended the territory of Anjou against her grandson Arthur of Brittany.

Louise de Savoie (1476–1531)

Louise de Savoie was the mother of sixteenth-century French king François I. A mother who liked to meddle in her son's business, she ruled the country while François was fighting in Italy, and again when he was captured and imprisoned by the Holy Roman Emperor Charles V.

She came into her own after François, who probably goes down in history as the most selfish father who ever lived, signed a treaty whereby he gave up certain territories then secured his own freedom in exchange for that of his two young sons, François and Henri, who were eight and six. As if that wasn't bad enough, he left them to rot in a Spanish jail for three years while he broke the treaty, ensuring that they would not be released.

While it is true that Louise had a hand in the incarceration of her poor, motherless grandchildren, she was also instrumental in their release. After discovering that their conditions were not as luxurious as they should've been, and that the king and Charles V had reached stalemate, she employed a dose of girl power.

She and daughter Marguerite approached the emperor's aunt and sister. If the men were too stubborn to budge, she reasoned, the women would have to sort out the mess themselves. The four met at Cambrai, northern France, on July 5, 1529, where they spent a month negotiating a treaty to end the war and ensure the safe return of François and Henri.

The resulting agreement was considered so fair and sensible that even the territorial males couldn't find fault with it. Happily, they signed the Treaty of Cambrai, which became known as *Les Paix des Dames* or "The Peace of the Ladies."

Josephine Baker (1906–1975)

The original Angelina Jolie, she adopted twelve children of varying ethnic backgrounds from around the world and called them her rainbow tribe.

Born Freda Josephine McDonald in Saint Louis, Missouri, she dropped out of school when she was twelve. In a time of segregation in the United States, Josephine overcame racism and discrimination to become one of the most successful performers of her day. A star of stage and screen, Josephine refused to play to segregated audiences and was instrumental in the integration of Las Vegas nightclubs.

Furthermore, she was decorated for her undercover work for the French Resistance during the Second World War and was the first American woman to receive French military honors at her Paris funeral.

If you've never been hated by your child,
you've never been a parent.
Bette Davis

Amy Hawkins

On April 17, 2006, a tornado ripped through Tennessee, claiming the lives of twelve residents. At the time, Amy Hawkins was at home with her two sons, six-year-old Jair and three-year-old Cole. As the tornado roared closer, she rushed them down to the basement. When the warning sounded, she lay on top of her boys while the family home was ripped apart, acting as a shield from falling debris. The boys were fine, but Amy was critically injured and rushed to hospital where she underwent emergency surgery on her back, which had been crushed.

As a result of her selfless bravery, she is now paralyzed from the hips down and may never walk again. In August 2006, the Hawkins family had their home rebuilt by the ABC show *Extreme Makeover* after public reaction to Amy's story made her a national celebrity.

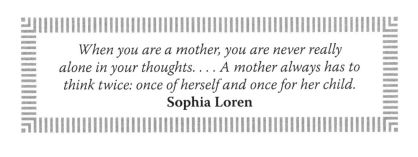

When you are a mother, you are never really alone in your thoughts. . . . A mother always has to think twice: once of herself and once for her child.
Sophia Loren

And Now for the Not So Heroic . . .

Ma Barker (1873–1935)

Kate "Ma" Barker was the matriarch of the notorious Karpis-Barker gang. During the Depression era, she and her sons, Herman, Lloyd, Arthur, and Fred, teamed up with criminal Alvin Karpis and several others and went on a four-year crime spree, that involved bank robberies, murders, and kidnappings.

In 1933, the gang kidnapped millionaire William Hamm, for whom they secured a ransom of $100,000. The following year, they abducted Minnesota banker Edward Bremer, Jr., whose ransom brought them $200,000.

Soon after, FBI agents created highly skilled "flying squads," specialized in hunting down the leading criminals and public enemies of the day. Ma Barker was gunned down by a flying squad in 1935, along with her son Fred.

At the time of the gang's brutal spree, Ma Barker was seen as the mastermind behind her boys' crimes. FBI chief J. Edgar Hoover believed she was as guilty as the men in every crime and a "veritable beast of prey."

Mama Rose (1892–1953)

Gypsy Rose Lee's mother featured heavily in the musical *Gypsy*, but it seems her loyal daughter was really quite kind to her mama and glossed over certain aspects of the family history to hide the faults of her terrible parent.

The original pushy stage mother, Rose Thompson Hovick first abandoned baby Rose and left her with relatives while she took her toddler June to Hollywood to star in silent films. Her preferred technique for making her child cry for the camera was to tell June that their dog had died.

At the age of seven, little Rose was taken out of school to join her mother and sister, and was taught to lie to truant officers if questioned. Mama Rose forced her daughters into vaudeville and threatened to give them away if they didn't do well. She trained them to steal from hotels and to leave restaurants without paying, and she once pushed a hotel manager out of a window.

Mama Rose even tried to shoot sixteen-year-old June's husband after having him arrested on false charges, but he escaped death only because when she pulled the trigger, the gun's safety was still on. It was also rumored that she shot her own boyfriend, although the official verdict was suicide.

Even when on her deathbed, legend has it that she was still controlling of her daughters. Her last words to Gypsy Rose Lee were allegedly, "Wherever you go, I'll be right there. When you get your own private kick in the [butt] just remember — it's a present from me to you."

What a gem!

Mother Nature

The maternal instinct is the most natural thing in the world. Our hormones make sure that in the vast majority of cases, we love each and every child we bring into the world, nurture them, and care for them in every way we can.

After all, Nature is a mother, so don't all female animals have a maternal instinct? Well, yes, although that instinct may work in some surprising ways.

Mothers of Dubious Character

Pandas

The cute, cuddly image of this black-and-white bear is something of an illusion when it comes to looking after its young. How often have we celebrated the birth of a panda cub in a zoo and marveled at the way the mother interacts with her offspring? The problem begins when the mother gives birth to twins — often she decides that one of the cubs is stronger and more likely to survive than the other, and then she completely abandons the weaker one! Motherly love can certainly be tough love!

Guinea Hens

The guinea hen is incredibly protective of her eggs, making a nest off the ground to guard them and keep them warm until they hatch. But it's when her babies start to hatch that the problem begins. The mother hen is up at first light to gather bugs, and the tiny chicks (or keets), inevitably try to follow their mom when she leaves the nest. As the nest is usually in a field, this invariably means trailing through long, often wet, grass. Unfortunately, Mom seems oblivious to the underdeveloped stature of her chicks and walks very fast, almost unaware that her babies are trying in vain to keep up. Although the mother's mission is clearly to find food for her brood, on the way quite a few of the exhausted chicks often fall away and die in the grass, leaving her with far fewer babies to feed than before she set out for food.

Penguins

Often thought to be among the best parents in nature for the protective way in which they nurture their eggs, penguins also have a heartless streak. Royal penguins, for example, lay two eggs in a season, the second being 60 percent larger than the first. Just before the second egg arrives, mom discards the first by rolling it out of the nest. Magellanic penguins hatch two eggs, and the mother then gives 90 percent of the fish she catches to one chick, ignoring the other's cries of hunger. The second one almost always dies.

Rabbits

What could be cuter than tiny baby bunnies? What rabbit mom could resist? Well, in some cases, they *can't* resist . . . eating them, that is. Some experts think this phenomenon is caused by stress, others believe it is because the doe simply doesn't understand what these small creatures are. Either way the result is not pretty!

African Black Eagles and Bald Eagles

The eagle can have two or three eaglets and will scour the countryside for food for her babies, often leaving the dad in charge. On her return, however, she will allow the strongest one or two of her young to hog all the food and then simply stand by and watch the stronger eaglet or eaglets peck a weaker sibling to death.

Mice

Like the rabbit, first-time moms will sometimes eat their own litter out of confusion or stress. They may also kill one or two of the weakest, as surviving in the wild can be difficult and a mommy mouse can't afford to nurture the ones that will straggle behind the rest.

Natural Mothers

Before you start to think that humans are the only ones who don't raise their children solely according to the laws of natural selection, here are a few of nature's most unconditionally caring mothers.

Whales, Porpoises, and Manatees

As mammals, these sea creatures nurse their young and keep them close at all times throughout the nursing period. They also make sure they nudge them to the surface at regular intervals for air. The baby swims close to its mother and is carried in the mother's "slip stream" and the mother becomes extremely aggressive if her baby is threatened. Don't we all?

Elephants

Elephant calves are among the luckiest offspring in nature. Not only do they get a great mom, but a whole herd of caring aunts as well. In the first year, when they are small enough to be trampled under the feet of their elders, the calf is in constant contact with its mom. If one strays more than twenty yards away, it will be retrieved. Weaning typically takes four or five years, but the bond is not then broken. A nine-year-old elephant still spends half its time within five yards of its mom. Interestingly enough, the males move away, but the bond between mother and daughter lasts up to fifty years. Closely related females look after one another's calves, sometimes even suckling them, and a baby elephant will drink more than ten quarts of milk a day! Now that's devotion to the sisterhood.

Alligators

Although they are cold-blooded, alligator moms appear to have warm hearts. An alligator lays between twenty and sixty eggs, which she then buries in a nest mound and protects fiercely throughout the two-month incubation period. When the eggs are ready to hatch, the mother digs into the nest mound, opens any eggs that have not hatched, and carries the young down to the water. Baby alligators stay close to their mom for the first two years, hibernating with her for the first year. During that time, you don't want to go near — she will defend them to the death.

Kangaroos

As a marsupial, the kangaroo has a built-in baby carrier. So immediately after birth, the lucky joey crawls up its mom's body and into a nice warm pouch. Inside, it attaches itself to one of four teats, which then enlarges to hold the baby in place. For the first few weeks, it has food on tap and is constantly warm. After that, the joey will make occasional forays away from the pouch and will leave after seven to ten months. While the males tend to go their own way when they are old enough, daughters stick close to their mothers for several years.

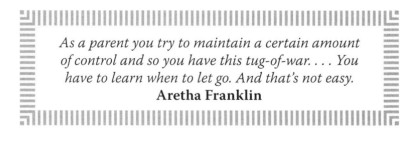

As a parent you try to maintain a certain amount of control and so you have this tug-of-war. . . . You have to learn when to let go. And that's not easy.
Aretha Franklin

How to Throw an Instant Dinner Party

(Or how to throw a party for your seven-year-old and his/her five friends with only two hours' notice)

When you arrive at your child's school for the afternoon pickup, your usual friendly smile turns into a frozen grin as your child runs out with the five friends he or she has generously invited over for dinner without telling you. Meanwhile, grateful mothers cheerfully wave their children good-bye (overjoyed to have some precious time to themselves) and arrange to pick them up later.

Of course, as a practiced goddess, you will be able to mask the rising panic within as you mentally count the number of chicken breasts you have left in the freezer.

After the initial fear of wondering how you'll feed all the little darlings, it's not long before some common sense and a bit of clever thinking kick in. Soon you're hosting the perfect instant party, and the children are eating out of your hands (not literally, hopefully). Here's how to do it.

1 **Distract the kids**
When friends are visiting, most kids are happy to run upstairs and put some serious effort into trashing their bedroom. If they, or you, are not thrilled with that idea, set up an art corner with pens, pencils, and (if you can stand the mess) paints, and sit the children down. Give them a snack of cheese, fruit, or yogurt first, so they don't whine about being hungry for the next hour or so.

2 **Forget the junk food and throw a party**
Finger food always goes down well, so here are a few suggestions for a quick, easy, and best of all, healthy party platter:

* Carrot and cucumber wedges

* String cheese

* Olives

* Cherry tomatoes

* Grapes

* Sliced apples

* Pizza (see recipes)

* Potato wedges (see recipe)

I know how to do anything — I'm a mom.
Roseanne Barr

Easy Pizza

For the base:
14 tbsp flour
1½ tsp dried yeast
1 egg, beaten
1 tsp salt
⅓ cup lukewarm tap water
½ tsp olive oil
1 tsp sugar

For the toppings:
1 medium can chopped tomatoes
or tomato puree
cheddar or mozzarella cheese

1. Whisk the water and sugar in a mixing bowl, and add the yeast. Leave 10–15 minutes until it is frothy.

2. Sift the flour and salt into another mixing bowl, then pour in the yeast and egg and a little water, if needed. Mix to a doughy consistency and knead for 10 minutes on a board or work surface. Put back into the bowl and cover with saran wrap or a damp cloth, then leave for an hour.

3. Meanwhile, mix the chopped tomatoes with a teaspoon of tomato puree. Then grate the cheddar or slice the mozzarella.

3 Place the dough in a shallow oblong baking pan 10 x 11 inches. Flatten and push out to the sides, then brush with olive oil. Spread the tomato mixture on top, followed by the cheddar or mozzarella, and bake at 425°F for 15–20 minutes.

Even Easier Pizza

This can be made with several types of breads that you may have in the house. Focaccia, ciabatta, and French bread work well, and so do pitas (especially mini ones) and even muffins or rolls.

1 Slice the bread lengthways (unless using pitas) and drizzle with a little olive oil.

2 Spread the tomato mixture from previous recipe on top, and top with ham, cooked bacon, or cooked chicken (optional), then with cheese.

3 Bake in a hot oven at 400°F until they are warm and the cheese has melted.

Healthy Potato Wedges

1. Peel, then cut the potatoes into large chunks and boil for ten minutes.

2. Drain and place on a baking tray.

3. Brush with oil and bake in the oven at 400°F for 25 minutes. Serve with ketchup.

Tuna Pasta

5.5 oz pasta shells
(or any pasta you have handy)
8 oz can of tuna
¾ cup cooked peas
1 tbsp plain flour
15.5 fl oz milk
4.5 oz grated cheese

1. Cook the pasta, drain and transfer to a greased oven dish. Mix in the tuna and peas.

2. Melt the butter in a saucepan and stir in the flour. Cook for a minute and stir in the milk until it thickens, then add half the grated cheese. Pour over the tuna and pasta and stir.

3. Spread the remaining cheese on top and dot with butter, then bake in a preheated oven at 450°F for about 15 minutes.

Chicken/Ham Wraps

1. Take a pack of tortillas and spread a little mayonnaise on each.

2. Add shredded lettuce, grated cheese, and diced cooked chicken or shredded ham, then roll into a wrap or fill a pita.

Sweet Treats

Why not get the kids involved in making their own dessert? It doesn't need to involve too much time or mess. Here are some simple recipes that the kids can help you with.

Easy Cereal Bars

1 large bar of milk chocolate
5.5 oz Rice Krispies or cornflakes
12 paper baking cups
1 wooden spoon
1 small Pyrex or metal bowl

1. Put some water in the saucepan and bring to a boil.

Place 13 squares of chocolate into the bowl (you can eat the rest!) and carefully place the bowl into the saucepan.

2 Put the Rice Krispies or cornflakes into a very large mixing bowl (kids have a tendency to mix roughly and make a terrible mess!). Pour the melted chocolate over the cereal and mix thoroughly, until all the cereal is covered.

3 Spoon the chocolate-coated cereal into the baking cups and leave to set for 15 minutes.

Banana Brûlée

4 ripe bananas
2 cups Greek yogurt
2 tbsp brown sugar

1 Peel and thinly slice the bananas, and place into four ramekin dishes. Top with the Greek yogurt and sprinkle a layer of sugar on top.

2 Place under a heated grill until they are golden and bubbling. Leave them to cool, but do not put them in the fridge.

3 Enjoy!

Things You'll Never Hear a Mother Say to Her Child

✳ Be good and I'll buy you a motorcycle!

✳ How on earth can you see the TV sitting so far back?

✳ Don't bother wearing a jacket — it's quite warm out.

✳ Let me smell that shirt.
Yes, that's good for another week.

✳ I think a messy bedroom is a sign of creativity.

✳ Yes, I used to play hooky, too.

✳ Just leave all the lights on.
It brightens things up!

✳ Could you turn the music up louder so I can enjoy it, too?

✳ Run and bring me the scissors! Hurry!

✳ Just turn your underpants inside out.
No one will ever know.

✳ No, I don't have a tissue with me — just use your sleeve.

The Heck with Housework

Ten Excuses Not to Do Housework

1. As soon as the kids get home, they'll undo all your hard work, anyway. As comedian Phyllis Diller put it so profoundly: "Cleaning your house while your kids are still growing is like shoveling the walk before it stops snowing."

2. Wit and raconteur Quentin Crisp had the right idea when he said, "There was no need to do any housework at all. After the first four years, the dirt doesn't get any worse."

3. Maid services can be very affordable. If you don't work and you can't bear the thought of watching someone else do your cleaning, grab some "me time" and go shopping or have lunch with a friend while someone else slaves away amid the dust and debris of your home.

4. You are unlikely to be appreciated for your effort, whereas a great new outfit and a makeover will make you feel better.

5. There's always tomorrow!

6 Make sure you have a friend who is messier than you. When you feel guilty because of the state of your house, go and visit her. You'll be amazed at how clean your house will seem when you get home.

7 If you have friends with immaculate houses, tell yourself that they must have too much time on their hands and lead a really boring life. You are *far* too interesting to spend all that time washing the windows, polishing the furniture, vacuuming the curtains, and scrubbing the kitchen floor.

8 Haven't you heard of *spring* cleaning? Once a year is enough.

9 Dust actually protects surfaces!

10 Frankly, there's always something better to do!

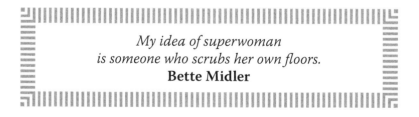

*My idea of superwoman
is someone who scrubs her own floors.*
Bette Midler

Ten Housework Shortcuts

1. If you have a dish-washer that gets gross and smelly, don't buy expensive cleaning products. Sprinkle a handful of baking soda in the bottom and set it to "wash" without any dishes inside.

2. Use a lint roller to dust the lamp shades.

3. Use the vacuum cleaner with a brush attachment to dust everything. Not only is it quicker than a duster, it actually sucks up the dust rather than just displacing it.

4. Alka-Seltzer makes a great cleaner for stained vases and thermoses. Drop in a couple of tablets and leave to soak for an hour or so before rinsing out. They are also effective cleaners of gold or silver jewelry. Put two tablets in a glass and then soak the jewelry for two minutes.

5. Place a cup of ammonia in your oven overnight and wipe the oven clean in the morning with a damp sponge. If you do this once a month, you will never have the horrible job

of scrubbing the baked-on grease from the inside of your oven. It's worth the few minutes a month.

6 Use white vinegar to remove grime in your bathroom.

7 To keep lint and dust off glass tabletops, wash them with a solution of warm water and fabric softener, using one tablespoon of liquid fabric softener to one quart of warm water. Not only is this cleaning solution inexpensive, it will help keep lint from gathering on the glass. It is also great for computer screens and TVs.

8 Bribe your kids to do the housework for you! If your daughter is old enough, tell her you are playing princesses and she is Cinderella. Then you can be the wicked step-mother and she'll be mopping the kitchen floor in no time! If you have a boy and a girl, try the Hansel and Gretel story. And if you have boys, have them pretend that they are soldiers and you are the drill sergeant.

9 Don't try to brush your pet's hair off the furniture. Just wipe the upholstery with a slightly dampened sponge.

10 And remember, never ever mix cleaning supplies. The results can be deadly!

Getting the Kids to Do Some Work

Bribing your children is often a successful method of motivating them to help you with the housework. To avoid getting caught up in aggressive price negotiations, however, work out a "fee" beforehand for each task. The table below is just an example; you may want to adjust the amounts to suit the age of your children.

* Emptying the dishwasher — $1.00

* Mopping the floor — $3.00

* Washing the dishes — $1.00

* Tidying up a room — $2.00

* Dusting a room — $2.00

* Vacuuming a room — $2.00

* Washing the car — $5.00

* Tidying their own room — nothing!
They should do that anyway.

Likely Excuses

*(Or things your children are bound to say,
and your likely response)*

But she started it!
I don't care who started it. *I'm* finishing it.

✳

I didn't do it!
Well, someone must have.

✳

It wasn't me!
Well, who was it then? Mr. Nobody?

✳

I don't want any more!
Think about the starving children!

Why can't I have it?
Because money doesn't grow on trees.

✳

Everyone else has one!
Is that right? Should I ask *everyone else's* mom?

✳

That's so unfair!
Life *is* unfair.

✳

Dad said I could have it!
Then Dad can pay for it.

✳

Johnny's mom lets him do it!
Good for Johnny's mom.

✳

Why?
Because I said so!

Kids' Kitchen

Children adore making things in the kitchen and, if you teach them well, they can even be a help.

There are few things as wonderful as the first time your child brings you a cup of coffee in bed. Then you know some of the hard work is over. Make sure you choose safe cooking activities, though, and always take the age of your child into consideration. After all, you don't want your four-year-old loose in the kitchen!

Always supervise your children, especially when liquids are boiling or something is in the oven, and keep the younger ones away from sharp knives.

Keep it fun, too, and don't get stressed if the cake mix gets smeared all over the counter or the dinner ends up on the floor!

Watercress Heads

Although this activity doesn't involve cooking, making watercress heads is one of the most fun and simple things to do in the kitchen. To start, you'll need some empty, intact eggshells. Carefully wash them out, then fill them with some damp cotton balls. Let the children draw funny faces on the shells with markers, but tell them to be gentle.

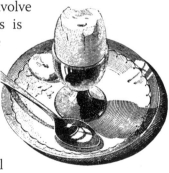

Next, sprinkle some watercress seeds on the cotton balls and put them aside. Watercress seeds will grow almost anywhere, but the best place is probably indoors on the windowsill where they will get the most sunlight. Encourage the children to keep the cotton balls damp by adding drops of water every day. After a few days, the funny faces will have spiky, edible green hair.

Toast Teddies

Easy and fun, this is a great snack for the kids to make.

You will need.
4 slices bread
some olive oil
a teddy bear–shaped cookie cutter

1. Use the cutter to make teddy bear shapes from the bread (the kids will love doing this part!)

2. Brush the teddy bears with olive oil and place in the oven for 5–6 minutes at 350°F until they are golden brown.

3. To serve, you can top them with just about anything: cheese, tomato, peanut butter, etc.

Alternatively, for a sweet version, leave out the olive oil and spread the bread with butter and honey before baking, and leave in the oven for 10 minutes. No extra topping is required.

Super Shakes and Smoothies

Bananarama

1 very ripe banana
¾ cup cold milk
2 tsp confectioners' sugar
or (preferably) honey
1 scoop ice cream
a blender

1. Put the whole banana in the blender or let your child chop it carefully with a butter knife before dropping it into the blender.

2. Add the sugar or honey to the banana and blend to a puree. Then add the milk and ice cream and blend again.

3. Pour into a tall glass and serve.

On special occasions you might want to add another scoop of ice cream on top with a sprinkle of grated chocolate. Yummy!

You can use the same method with any canned fruit and most berries. Strawberries and raspberries taste particularly good in smoothies.

Salad Days

Children will always be able to help you prepare a salad, even if they can't use a sharp knife. Let them wash the lettuce, and if you have a salad spinner, they will enjoy drying it, too. Let them chop up things that aren't too tough, like hard-boiled eggs, but steer clear of giving them a sharp knife to tackle the carrots!

To make it more fun, try cutting silly shapes out of carrots, cucumbers, etc.

Lassi Come Home

For a healthy drink, blend equal quantities of plain yogurt and milk with some honey. Add fruit if you wish.

This drink is called Lassi and is served with many meals in India. It is particularly good if your child has a mild stomachache.

Time for Something a Little Bit Harder

When your child has mastered the basics, and you have mastered the art of not pulling your hair out when it all goes wrong, you could try some of the following. But don't worry, it's not rocket science!

Yummy Cupcakes

For those of us who didn't grow up around a cake-baking, jam-making kitchen queen, the word *baking* can strike fear into our very core. Just remember — no one will know the difference if you use store-bought cake mix!

Children love to make cakes, and, for the younger ones, the mixing bowl provides most of the fun. The instructions are simple enough for all ages and the results are delicious. If you have visitors to share with, you can always lie and say it was all your own work!

However, if you want to start from scratch, the easiest recipe is for cupcakes. To make a dozen cupcakes you will need:

5 tbsp softened butter
7½ tbsp superfine sugar
2 eggs
8 tbsp self-rising flour
2 tbsp milk
12 paper baking cups

For the icing:
7½ tbsp confectioners' sugar
1–2 tbsp warm water

1. Beat the butter and sugar together until fluffy and light. Add one egg and stir in until the mixture is creamy and smooth, then add the second egg and do the same.

2. Sieve the flour into the mixture, then add the milk and beat together.

3. Pour the mixture into the 12 paper-lined muffin cups.

4. Bake in the oven for 15–20 minutes at 350°F, and then leave to cool on a wire rack.

5. For the icing, mix the confectioners' sugar with 1–2 tbsp of warm water and spread over the cooled-down cupcakes.

Let the kids decorate them as they wish. They can use jelly beans, or M&Ms. Or they can make funny faces using colored icing and cake decorations.

Flapjack Fun

These sweet treats are delicious — and a favorite with most kids. They also contain fruit and oats, so they're not too unhealthy either.

1½ cups oats
3 tbsp sugar
2 tbsp butter or margarine
2 tbsp golden syrup
¾ cup dried fruit (e.g. sliced apricots, raisins, mixed fruit)
a shallow baking tin

1. Grease a shallow baking tin.

2. Place the sugar, butter, and syrup into a saucepan and heat on low until the butter has melted. Then stir in the oats.

3. Pour half of the mixture into the baking tin and arrange the dried fruit over the oat mixture. Then pour the remaining mixture over the fruit and pat down.

3. Bake for 20 minutes at 400°F or until lightly browned.

4. Remove from the oven and cut into portions in the baking tin while hot. Use an oven mitt to hold the tin steady. Try not to burn yourself — and don't let a young child help with this part!

Supercool Sandwiches

Kids love making their own sandwiches, but you may find that they get bored with traditional ingredients. Try combining a few different things to make their sandwiches more interesting.

✳ Tuna and egg

✳ Egg and corn

✳ Peanut butter and cucumber

✳ Avocado and chicken

✳ Mozzarella and tomato
(this is even better if lightly toasted)

✳ Ham and cheese

✳ Bacon, lettuce, and tomato (BLT)

Also, try some different breads such as focaccia, ciabatta, and pita.

Sailboat Sandwiches

These snacks are a lot of fun to make because they look like yachts and taste great. You will need:

oval-shaped rolls such as sub rolls
peanut butter, tuna salad, cream cheese
or other sticky ingredients
1 banana (if using peanut butter)
or corn (if using tuna)
sliced cheddar cheese

1. Slice the roll in half to make two boat shapes, and spread the sticky ingredients on the exposed part of the roll to cover the middle section of the "boat."

2. Use another ingredient, such as banana or corn, to create a rim around the edge of the "deck."

3. Finally, make a sail for the sailing ship by putting a toothpick through some sliced cheddar cheese or ham and stand it in the middle of the boat.

These sandwiches are great for parties or just for a fun lunch.

A Mother's Wisdom

(Or things your mother told you . . .
and the scientific truth)

"If you swallow chewing gum, it will stay in your digestive system for seven years."

The Truth: Chewing gum, like anything else, stays in your digestive system for an average of about twenty hours as roughage.

*

"If you don't wait an hour after eating to go swimming, you will get a cramp and drown."

The Truth: No death has ever been attributed to entering a pool too quickly after eating, although a huge meal, followed by excessive exercise, could cause cramping or indigestion.

*

"One hundred strokes with a brush is good for your hair."

The Truth: This myth came about when people rarely washed their hair, but now that we wash our hair more frequently, the opposite is true. Excessive brushing wears away the hair's cuticle making it more matted and tangly, and causing split ends.

**"Your hair will grow back thicker and darker
after you've shaved it."**

The Truth: Hair may seem to grow back thicker because
short hairs tend to feel and look dark and coarse,
but it's just an illusion.

✳

**"If you make ugly faces, your face will stay that way
if the wind changes."**

The Truth: Clearly, there is no scientific basis
for this old wives' tale!

"Sweets will rot your teeth."

The Truth: Obviously there's some truth to this (and we
wouldn't advise telling your children it's not true!), but some
carbohydrates such as pasta and soft breads can do more
damage than sugar because acid is formed by the food rem-
nants in the mouth. Saliva can fully dissolve sugar, but not
these fermentable carbohydrates.

"Eat your carrots — they're good for your eyes."

The Truth: The beta-carotene in carrots is an excellent source of vitamin A, and a deficiency of this vitamin causes night blindness. But in developed countries, vitamin A deficiency is virtually nonexistent.

※

"If you eat the crusts on your bread, they'll make your hair curl."

The Truth: Although crusts are good for you, because the browning reaction on the surface of the bread produces antioxidants, there is no evidence to suggest that eating them has any effect on your hair!

※

"If you go out with wet hair, you'll catch a cold."

The Truth: You may well feel colder if you go outside with wet hair, but that won't make you any more likely to catch a cold. Viruses cause colds and getting cold doesn't.

※

"Chicken soup is good for colds."

The Truth: This is actually true because chicken soup is thought to boost the immune system by stopping the movement of white blood cells that stimulate the release of mucus. It's also packed with nutrition, is easy to swallow, and will help keep you hydrated. Not to mention that it's a tasty comfort food (as long as you're not a vegetarian)!

"Stop cracking your knuckles — you'll get arthritis."

The Truth: This is a myth, although knuckle cracking can lead to cartilage damage.

✳

"If you're pregnant and your 'bump' is all in the front, you'll have a boy."

The Truth: The shape of your bump has more to do with the position of the baby than its sex. If its back is facing away from the mom's spine, it's more likely to stick out in the front.

"An apple a day keeps the doctor away."

The Truth: Any fresh fruit, eaten on a regular basis, helps to keep you healthy. Apples, in particular, are good sources of flavonoids, which might have anticarcinogenic effects.

✳

"Feed a cold, starve a fever."

The Truth: If you have a fever, your metabolism increases and you burn energy more quickly. This means you require more food and fluids. Feeding a cold will have no beneficial effect unless it is with food rich in vitamin C.

Mum's the Word

Anecdotes and stories about mothers

Minnie, the mother of the Marx Brothers, had a sense of humor to match that of her sons. "Because we were a kid act, we traveled at half-fare, despite the fact that we were all around twenty," Groucho once recalled. "Minnie insisted we were thirteen."

"'That kid of yours is in the dining car smoking a cigar,' the conductor told her. 'And another one is in the washroom shaving.' Minnie shook her head sadly and said, 'They grow so fast!'"

One morning while studying in Australia, Prince Charles attended a service at the local parish church. The rector spoke to the prince after the service and apologized for the small turnout.

"Being bank holiday weekend," he explained, "most of the parishioners are away."

"Not another bank holiday!" the prince exclaimed. "What's this one?"

"Well," the rector replied, rather embarrassed, "over here we call it the Queen's birthday."

Charlie Chaplin grew up in poverty in South London. When he rose to fame he adopted his famous tramp costume as his trademark. The first time his mother saw him wearing it she exclaimed, "Charlie, I have to get you a new suit!"

✳

Johnny Depp likes to remember events in his life with a tattoo. Among the reminders on his body he has Wino Forever, which used to say Winona Forever, but was altered when he split with former fiancée Winona Ryder. He also has a Cherokee chief on his right arm and his mother's name, Betty Sue, tattooed on his left

✳

In *Oliver Twist* (1922), Jackie Coogan was required to cry on cue. When asked "Where's your mother?" he had to reply, "My mother is dead, sir," and burst into tears. However, the eight-year-old actor couldn't force himself to cry. Frank Lloyd, the film's director, suggested that he try to imagine that his mother really was dead, but still the tears refused to come. Suddenly, the young Jackie had an idea. "Mr. Lloyd," he said, "would it be all right if I imagine my dog is dead?"

✳

At the tender age of six, Shirley Temple stopped believing in Santa Claus. "Mother took me to see him in a department store," she later explained. "He asked for my auto-graph, and said he saw all my movies."

"Me Time" for Moms: Perfect Pampering

When you've spent all day running around after your demanding brood, it's time to treat yourself like a princess and enjoy a bit of self-pampering. Trying to fit everything into your busy schedule is exhausting and, let's face it, being the perfect mom you are, your need for a good time is usually last on the list of priorities. But "me time" is a must if you're going to preserve your

sanity and maintain your role as supermom.

Pamper Parties

Trying to have a social life, get a manicure, and find time to relax is very difficult, but this activity kills three birds with one stone. There are various companies that provide this service and you can get information about them by asking in your local beauty salon or searching online.

Any mother could perform the jobs of several air-traffic controllers with ease.
Lisa Alther

When you've found a pampering service that suits your needs, call a group of friends and invite them to your house (making sure that all male partners are out of the way for the day), then prepare the living room with scented candles and snacks. The beautician will do the rest. You can get everything from massages to manicures, pedicures, and facials, as well as sharing some good gossip with your friends. If all goes well, you'll find yourself in an unbelievably relaxed state of mind by the end of the evening.

Get a Haircut

Looking better makes you feel better, so if you haven't changed your hairstyle for a while, book an appointment with a good hairdresser and go for it. It might only take an hour, but it makes all the difference.

Soak It All Away

Though it's a cliché, a long, hot bath can relax you in a way that no other activity can. The ancient Greek and Romans used hydrotherapy to cure stress, aches, and anxiety, and it is still used in medicine today. Light some scented

candles and add some aromatherapy oil or bubble bath to the water — then soak up the benefits.

In *The Bathtub Yoga and Relaxation Book,* author Margaret Jaffe says, are of yourself, and [a bath] teaches you to take time, meditate and be mindful of your body." It's also nice to be in a room with a locked door.

The Dating Game

She may be a working mother with two children, but Michelle Pfeiffer still "dates" her husband, David E. Kelley. "David and I have date nights when we go out to the movies," she says. "It's

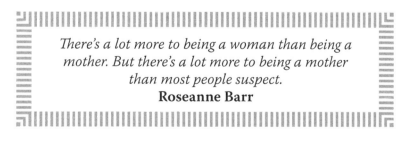

There's a lot more to being a woman than being a mother. But there's a lot more to being a mother than most people suspect.
Roseanne Barr

one of my favorite things to do and it helps keep the marriage alive." But if you can't get a babysitter, why not bring the theater to your living room. Buy some popcorn, dim the lights, and rent a DVD — then snuggle up with your partner and relax.

If movies aren't your thing, re-create a favorite vacation destination in your own home. If you love Italy, for example, cook a special pasta dinner, lay a checked tablecloth with scented candles, and reminisce about a romantic vacation that you both shared. If you don't have a partner, do something similar with the kids. It will be a refreshing change from routine.

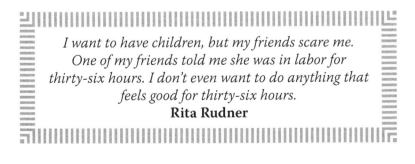

I want to have children, but my friends scare me.
One of my friends told me she was in labor for
thirty-six hours. I don't even want to do anything that
feels good for thirty-six hours.
Rita Rudner

Things My Mother Taught Me

My mother taught me about patience . . .
"Just wait until your father gets home!"

My mother taught me about receiving . . .
"You are really going to get it when we get home!"

My mother taught me to meet a challenge . . .
"What were you thinking? Answer me when I talk to you! Don't talk back to me!"

My mother taught me logic . . .
"If you fall out of that swing and break your neck, you're not going shopping with me!"

My mother taught me medical science . . .
"If you sit too close to the TV, you will become cross-eyed!"

My mother taught me to think long-term . . .
**"If you don't pass your spelling test,
you'll never get a good job."**

My mother taught me about ESP . . .
**"Put your sweater on; don't you think
I know when you're cold?"**

My mother taught me humor . . .
"When you break a leg, don't come running to me."

My mother taught me about genetics . . .
"You're just like your father."

My mother taught me about my roots . . .
"You weren't born in a fish tank, you know!"

My mother taught me about the wisdom of age . . .
"When you get to be my age, you will understand!"

My mother taught me about justice . . .
**"One day you'll have kids, and I hope they turn out
just like you. . . . Then you'll see what it's like."**

*The joys of motherhood are never fully
experienced until the children are in bed.*
Author unknown

Halloween Queen

Halloween is a favorite holiday among children, and getting into the spirit doesn't have to take all your money or time. To throw the best Halloween party in town, all you need are a few shortcuts and a spooky sense of humor!

Frightening Food

Use a cookie cutter to make ghost-shaped cookies or witches' hats.

＊

Scoop out the insides of a pumpkin and fill it with bug- and snake-shaped candy. It looks especially gross if they're spilling out over the sides.

Slice the top off of an orange, scoop out the insides, and carve a face on one side. Then fill the orange with ice cream, and put the top back on. The icy oranges can be kept in the freezer until it's time to eat them.

Spider Cakes

Ice some cupcakes (see p. 60 for recipe) with chocolate frosting and add black licorice for legs. Jelly beans make great eyes too, and you can decorate the cupcakes with other candy if you want to make your spider more colorful.

Eggy Eyeballs

1 Make some hard-boiled eggs and wait for them to cool.

2 Slice each one in half, widthwise, scoop out the yolk and fill the holes with cream cheese.

3 Add a pimento-stuffed olive, which has been sliced in half with the pimento showing.

4 Then dip a toothpick in red food coloring and draw veiny lines across the white of the eggs to make them look really bloodshot.

Evil Eggs

These eggs look especially real when prepared a day in advance.

1. Make some hard-boiled eggs and cool them in cold water.

2. Crack the shells all over with the back of a spoon, making sure not to break any pieces of egg off.

3. Place the eggs in a bowl of cold water with a tablespoon of food coloring (whichever color you prefer) and leave them for eight hours or overnight.

4. Remove the shells and place the colored eggs in a nest of grated carrot and shredded lettuce.

Creepy-crawly Jell-O

1. Buy some gummy worms and place them in the bottom of a glass bowl. Then make half a package of Jell-O and pour the liquid on top of the gummies.

2. When the Jell-O has set, add some more gummy worms and cover with the remaining Jell-O.

A word of warning — don't leave the Jell-O for too long after making it, as the candies tend to swell up!

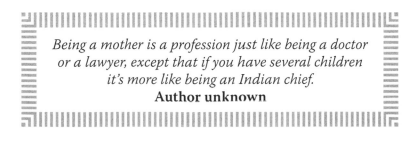

Being a mother is a profession just like being a doctor or a lawyer, except that if you have several children it's more like being an Indian chief.
Author unknown

Hot Frogs

1. Roll out some puff pastry and use a frog-shaped cutter, or make a frog-shaped template to cut around, to create some frog shapes measuring approximately 5.5 x 5 inches, then place them on a baking sheet and prick their tummies gently with a fork

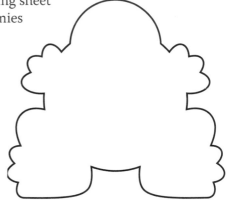

2. Take some green apples and cut them in half, cutting out the core and seeds. Fill the hollow with raisins soaked in orange juice.

3. Brush the pastry frogs with some milk or soft butter, and place half an apple on each frog's tummy, skin side up.

3. Use raisins for their eyes, then bake the pastry frogs for 15–20 minutes at 375°F, until golden.

4. Serve with green ice cream.

Easy-to-make Halloween Costumes

Batwear

To make this simple costume, all you need is a black leotard or a tight-fitting black T-shirt and tights, and some black felt for the bat wings.

1. Take a large piece of black felt and cut out two large bat-wing shapes, making sure that the length of the wing measures the same as the distance from your child's wrist to the top of his/her shoulder.

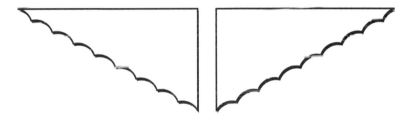

2. Sew loops of black elastic to the underside of each wing (make sure they're large enough for your child's wrists to fit through), and then sew or pin the other end of the bat wings to the back of the leotard or T-shirt.

3. To make a simple hood, measure your child's head from his/her forehead over the top to the back of the neck, then measure the distance from one ear to the middle of the back of the head. Take a piece of black felt and use the two measurements when drawing two hood shapes on the material and four bat-ear shapes (see suggested shapes on next page) and then cut them out.

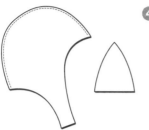

④ Sew the two hood shapes together with the furry sides touching, then turn inside out. Now, sew two of each of the ear pieces together, leaving a gap at the bottom that is wide enough to fit an ear-shaped piece of cardboard. The cardboard should make the bat ears more rigid before they are attached to the hood.

⑤ Next, sew the ears in place on the sides of the hood, and add a strip of Velcro at the chin to help the hood stay on.

Trash Troll

This is a simple, convincing costume that doesn't require any sewing!

① Take a black tie-top trash bag and cut armholes just below the ties. Then cut off the base of the bag in a zigzag pattern. Lengthwise it should hang above your child's feet.

② Using leaf stencils, either store-bought or cut from stiff cardboard with a craft knife, spray overlapping leaf designs in bright, autumnal colors on the trash bag.

③ When the paint has dried, put the costume on a willing child, drawing the strings loosely around his/her neck and tying them into a bow.

④ Add tights or leggings, then mess up your child's hair and color with spray-on (nonpermanent) dye and firm-hold hairspray to make it look nice and wild. Brown face paint can also be added, to look like smeared dirt. It's probably the only time you'll let your kids get away with looking so messy, so let them enjoy the moment!

Please note: This costume is not recommended for very young children due to the risk of suffocation or choking.

Wicked Queen

① Fold a large piece of purple or red felt in half and cut out a basic cape shape (see p. 20).

② Then cut vertical slits below the neckline and run enough ribbon through to tie into a bow around the neck.

③ Add three 2.5-inch-wide strips of fake fur across the top and down the sides of the cape using fabric glue.

④ Dress your child in a black outfit, such as a black top, skirt, and tights.

⑤ For a wicked crown, cut a piece of black cardboard into a crown and glue on colorful plastic gems.

⑥ Add costume jewelry and finish with wicked fake nails, spooky makeup, and a wand.

Count Dracula

1. Create a cape out of black felt (see p. 20).

2. Slick back hair and add fake fangs.

3. Use white face makeup to make the skin look pale and a black eyebrow pencil to create some arched brows and a pointed hairline, then add a dab of red lipstick to the lips.

Scary Mummy

1. Wrap your little one in bandages (or strips of old white sheets), leaving the face bandage-free.

2. As a finishing touch, cover the face with white makeup. What could be easier?

The Hunchback of Notre Dame

1. Create a hunchback by stuffing a small sofa pillow under a baggy T-shirt.

2. Find an old coat several sizes too large to wear over the humpbacked shirt.

3. Add some baggy pajama bottoms and a straggly wig.

Halloween Games

Apple Bobbing

First, tie a long piece of string, horizontally from two fixed objects (perhaps a banister or a coatrack), above head height. Then, using some apples with sturdy stems, tie smaller lengths of string to each apple stem and fasten the other end to the horizontal string, making sure that each apple dangles close to the children's heads. The kids must try to bite the apples without using their hands. If you'd prefer to do this outdoors, you could hang the apples on an unused clothesline.

Wrap the Mummy

Divide the kids into two teams and choose a "mummy." Then provide each team with a roll of toilet paper and tell them to "wrap the mummy." The first team to wrap their mummy, with just the eyes and nose showing, is the winner.

Touchy-Feely Scary Story

You will need:
a large cardboard box
a pumpkin
a feather
a small plush toy
some twigs
some Jell-O
fresh peeled grapes
cold spaghetti

Cut a hole in the front and back of a large cardboard box, so that you can place each item inside from the back, as it is mentioned in the story, hiding it under a cloth so that it can't be seen as it is moved into place.

Turn the lights down low and tell a scary story, getting the children to put their hands into the front of the box and feel each item when it's mentioned in the story. You can make up your own story or use this one. You can also use some of the guests' names if you like.

In a deep, dark cave, in a deep, dark woods, lived a wicked, old witch.

One night, as a full moon rose in the sky, Georgia and Joe were walking through the deep, dark woods on their way home. Playing together happily, Joe ran into the trees and his sister chased him, deeper and deeper until, suddenly, they realized they were lost.

Suddenly feeling frightened, Joe began to cry, but his

big sister put on her bravest face. "We'll be fine, Joe," she said. "Let's find somewhere to sleep until the morning, when it's light, and we'll be able to find our way home."

At that moment, Georgia spotted a cave. "In here, Joe," she said. "This will do."

But as they entered the cave, the children could hear an eerie whisper. They reached out their hands and touched the slimy wall (**the lid of the pumpkin**). Then, slowly, they moved inside the cave and Joe put his hand on a rock. Wriggling worms moved between his fingers (**cooked spaghetti**). Joe backed away just as something crawled across Georgia's hand (**feather**).

The children were really frightened, but something was calling them into the cave. The whispers were getting louder. Suddenly, they felt something furry brush against them (**plush toy**). They screamed as a cat ran away into the cave. As soon as it had gone, a faint light could be seen at the end of a dark tunnel.

"Let's see what it is," said Georgia, who was too curious to be afraid now. Teeth chattering, Joe followed her down the corridor. As they got closer to the light, though, it grew dim and a cackle was heard in the gloom.

"Come in, children," said an old woman's voice. "I won't bite." A loud cackle split the air again.

Georgia and Joe reached out and touched the woman's bony finger (**twig**).

"It's all right, children," she cackled again. "Come in and have something to eat."

Joe, who loved his food, moved forward into a round chamber where a little fire glowed. On the fire sat a cauldron, and sitting beside it glaring, was a black cat.

The old lady offered the children three dishes but it was too dark to see, so they touched the food in each dish.

First they felt something hard (**small twigs**). "What's this?" they asked.

"Bats' claws," answered the witch quietly.

Then they felt something squishy (**Jell-O**). "What's that?" they asked.

"Toads' intestines," answered the witch quietly.

Next they felt something round and squishy (**peeled grapes**). "What's this?" they asked.

"EYEBALLS," shouted the witch.

The children screamed and then ran and ran until they reached the other side of the woods where they found their mom and dad, who had been very worried about them and were out looking for them. Not surprisingly, Georgia and Joe never went into the woods again!

THE END

Record-breaking Moms

Anything we can do, they can do better! If you think you've had a big baby, or more children than you can shake a stick at, take a look at this impressive bunch.

The record for the most children born to one woman is a staggering sixty-nine. The wife of an eighteenth-century Russian peasant was reported to have been pregnant twenty-seven times, giving birth to sixteen sets of twins, seven sets of triplets, and four sets of quadruplets.

✳

The heaviest baby ever born was to Canadian Anna Bates in 1879. Her baby boy weighed 23 pounds 12 ounces. Ouch!

American mothers Laura Shelley and Caroline Cargado share a record achievement. Both women have had two sets of twins who share the same birthday. Laura gave birth to Melissa Nicole and Mark Fredrick Julian Jr. in 1990, followed by Kayla May and Jonathan Price Moore in 2003, both on March 25. Caroline had Keilani Marie and Kahleah Mae in 1996, then Mikayla Anee and Malia Abigail in 2003, both on May 30.

*

Lisa Coffey, from Virginia, is the proud mother of the lightest surviving triplets ever. Born by emergency Caesarean on November 30, 1998, they had a combined weight of 48.75 ounces. Peyton weighed in at 1 pound 4.5 ounces, Jackson 14.75 ounces, and Blake 13.5 ounces. The babies spent nearly four months in the hospital before they were allowed home, but they are now fit, healthy kids — and no doubt quite a handful.

*

Maddalena Granata, from Nocera, Italy, was born in 1839, married at twenty-eight, and gave birth to fifteen sets of triplets. In total, she had fifty-two children, forty-nine of whom were boys.

Mary Jonas of the United Kingdom (who died in 1899)
gave birth to fifteen sets of twins, all of whom were
a boy-girl combination.

✳

The oldest woman to have become a mother is Adriana Iliescu
of Romania. After undergoing fertility treatment, she gave birth
to a baby girl in January 2005, at the age of sixty-six. "Each
person has a mission in life, and maybe this was my mission," said the happy mom on the birth of Eliza Maria. Dr.
Bogdan Marinescu, who carried out the fertility treatment,
earlier justified the procedure by saying Adriana was in good
enough health to give birth. But the birth of Eliza led to calls
by Romanian officials for a public debate on the medical and
ethical implications of fertility treatments.

✳

Dr. Patricia Rashbrook caused controversy when she became
the oldest woman in the United Kingdom to give birth, at
the age of sixty-two. Dr. Rashbrook, who had three grown
children from a previous marriage, traveled to Eastern Europe
to receive fertility treatment from Italian expert Severino

Antinori and, in May 2006, gave birth to a healthy 6-pound 10.5-ounce boy, nicknamed J.J. She dismissed her critics and declared, "He is adorable, and seeing him for the first time was beyond words. Having been through so much to have him, we are overjoyed. His birth is absolutely wonderful." Should the age of his mother cause J.J. any anxiety when he gets older, at least she will be qualified to deal with it: Dr. Rashbrook is a child psychiatrist.

On July 25, 1978, Lesley Brown gave birth to a 5-pound 12-ounce daughter and made history. The baby, Louise Joy Brown, was the world's first IVF baby. Lesley and husband, John, had been trying to conceive for nine years, but in 1977 help appeared in the form of a new medical procedure called in vitro fertilization. The Browns participated in the experiment and Louise was the happy result. Since Louise's birth, millions of babies have been born using IVF. Happily she is now a mom herself, having conceived naturally.

Oh, Mom!

(Or things you should never do when you're a mom)

Make your children's clothes.

✳

Wear your children's clothes.

✳

Make your child wear hand-me-downs that are too big, too small, or contain holes.

✳

Make your daughter wear her big brother's hand-me-downs.

✳

Say "I told you so" when your child falls off the chair he/she has been standing on and cracks his/her head open.

Cut your child's hair.

✻

Make your children kiss terrifying old relatives.

✻

Show naked baby photos of your teenage son to his friends or girlfriend.

Rainy Day Play

You've just promised the kids they can go to the park, when you pull back the curtains and see sheets of rain falling from the skies. You'll need to think quickly to stem the flow of wailing and protesting from your little gems, who just can't seem to understand why rain should stop play.

But all is not lost. With a little imagination and a lot of patience, a wet afternoon can be fun for everyone.

Recyclable Sculptures

This needs some advance planning, such as saving cereal boxes, liquid soap containers, and empty paper towel rolls. Other useful containers, include Pringles tubes, egg cartons, and yogurt cups.

Grab as many empty containers as you can get your hands on and put them in a pile in the middle of a table. Spread out sheets of newspaper underneath, so the kids can make as much of a mess as they want, and provide them with child-safe glue, scissors, and tape. With your preparation work done, it's now up to the kids to use their imaginations to create a masterpiece. The only drawback is that once your children have presented you with the car/rocket/bus that they have lovingly made, you will be forced to treat it as a Rodin sculpture, put it on display, and promise *never* to throw it away. Of course, if you let enough time pass, you can hide it and, eventually, when they've forgotten about it, consign it to the trash can.

Home Theater

Rather than sticking them in front of the TV, make a theater experience in your own living room. Rent a new video or DVD, or find an old one you haven't seen in a while, then draw the curtains and turn out the lights.

Popcorn and soft drinks will make it feel more like a movie theater, and, if you have a popcorn popper or a microwave, making the popcorn can be part of the fun. If your children don't like popcorn, cut up pieces of fruit and put them in a popcorn bucket or large drinking cup.

OK, so they're still sitting in front of the TV, but at least you've put some thought into it!

Smart Charts

Ask your children to make a chart about themselves. Each chart should contain the name and age of the child and some personal details, such as height, hair color, and eye color. Then they can add a list of their favorite things, including favorite color, TV program, and song.

They'll have tons of fun making the charts, and, if they make them regularly, the charts will be a great way of seeing how your child changes as he/she grows up. Keep them all stored somewhere safe and, when they are older, you can spend another rainy afternoon going through them together.

Designer T-shirt

Kids love to decorate clothing and they will enjoy wearing their creations. Give each child a light-colored, plain T-shirt and a packet of fabric crayons or paints, which can be bought in most big supermarkets or in a craft store. Stretch the T-shirt over a large piece of cardboard to create a nice, flat surface.

For the best results, make sure the kids work out their design on a piece of paper first, otherwise you might end up with a designer disaster that nobody in their right mind would wear.

Dress-up Day

When you clear out the wardrobe you may want to throw most of your clothes away or give them to the local charity, but keep a few choice items aside to use for dressing up.

Dresses and skirts are ideal, as well as a few loose tops, old jewelry, and the occasional pair of pants. If you can spare the space, put them in an old suitcase or a toy box, and now the kids have the makings for an instant game of dress-up on any rainy day.

If you add a few wigs and old hats that you've picked up cheaply at a local thrift store, the resulting hilarity will be well worth it!

Taste Test

Select eight different foods and put them in small bowls. Then label them with numbers 1 to 8. Some of the best foods to use include yogurt, chocolate mousse, mashed banana, oatmeal, tomato sauce, salad dressing, and jam.

Allow each child to taste a tiny spoonful from each bowl and write down (or tell you, if they are too young to write) what they think each one is. This works better if you blindfold them. The winner is the one who guesses the most correctly.

Treasure Hunt

Hide gifts or treats around the house for each child, and lay a trail of clues. Each clue should lead to another until the final hiding place is found, but make sure that you take each child's age into account.

To make it more fun (for you as well as them), try writing the clues in rhyme. For example:

By a mirror, near a door,
You will find clue number four.

Are We There Yet?

Children love going on vacations and trips, but for every outing there is the inevitable and dreaded car ride! Sitting in a traffic jam on a hot day with two or three restless children in the back is not many people's idea of fun, but it doesn't need to be the worst part of the day.

The best way to survive the experience is to make it fun. Let the children each pack a bag of snacks, but make sure they  don't eat them all at once — the only thing worse than sitting in a traffic jam with bored kids is five hours in a car with a child who's sick to his stomach.

Once you've got your directions sorted out, pass the time with some car games. It really will make the trip seem quicker and should make the experience a lot less stressful for you!

Car Bingo

Before you set off, take some sheets of paper and write or draw a selection of objects for the children to look out for. Choose all the things that they are likely to see on the trip, such as stoplights, road signs, semi trucks, and gas stations, making each card slightly different. As they spot each object, they can tick it off on their card. The first to see all the objects shouts out "Bingo" and is the winner.

Alternatively, you will find that there are various Web sites that have already done the work for you. Just print off the sheets and away you go.

Twenty Questions

One player thinks of a noun that falls in the category of either person, place, or thing, and he/she then tells the other players which of these it is. Everyone else then takes turns asking questions to which the first player can only answer yes or no. If the others do not guess the object before twenty questions have been asked, the first player is the winner. If the object is guessed, the player who guesses correctly is the next to go.

For very young children who might not understand the concept of person, place, or thing, it may be better to limit the game to animals.

Who Am I?

Who Am I? is exactly the same as Twenty Questions except that the first player has to think of a famous person, who can be anyone from Abraham Lincoln to Madonna. The other players then ask yes or no questions such as "Are you still alive?" and "Are you male?" and the first to guess the person correctly is the winner.

The Fat Cat Game

This is a surprisingly simple but amusing game. A player thinks of a rhyming adjective and noun, such as "fat cat" or "black sack," and then gives a simple clue. The others must then guess the phrase. For example, the clue for "fat cat" could be "chubby feline."

Geography

This game is best for children seven years and older. The first player names a country and the next player then must think of another one that begins with the last letter of the first. For example, if player one says Canada, the next could say Australia, and so on. The game continues until someone is stumped and then they are out. The last person who is still in after everyone else has failed to keep thinking up new countries is the winner.

Although this is traditionally played with country names, you can adapt it to almost anything. It can be place names, book characters, or even music groups.

Connections

A simple word game that relies on quick reactions, one player thinks of a random word and the next person must think of a connecting word (a word that is somehow related to the first word) as quickly as he/she can. For example, player one might say "snow," player two "cold," and player three "hot." Anyone who hesitates, repeats a word that has already been used, or chooses an unconnected word is out.

Make Up a Story

Player one starts with a sentence about absolutely anything, for example, "Johnny was walking through the park when he saw . . ." The next person has to finish the sentence. For example, ". . . a one-legged chicken!" It's a great game for encouraging the children's imagination to run wild, and the stories are bound to be hilarious.

Teen Trouble

OK, so not everything gets easier as the kids get older. Suddenly, your sweet little angel turns into a growling, incomprehensible lump who won't move from the sofa. Footballs and action figures give way to smelly socks and acne, and Barbie dolls are ousted for makeup and celebrity pinups.

When you are having the eighteenth argument of the day, don't forget that much of it is the result of hormones — and who understands those better than a mom? Remember all the mood swings you went through when you were younger, because of pregnancy or PMS? It's payback time!

What Your Teenager Isn't Telling You

She's cheerful, helpful, and never far from the phone.
She's in love.

✳

He blushes at the mention of a certain name, or the mere suggestion of a girlfriend.
He's in love.

✳

She's moping around, won't leave the bedroom, and doesn't want to talk to anyone but her friends.
She's been dumped.

He thinks girls are a waste of time
and football/computer games are much better.
He's been dumped.

She asks if she can use the home phone to call a friend.
She has used all her cell phone minutes again.

*

He says, "I'd rather walk. It's good exercise."
when you offer him a ride.
He's embarrassed to be seen with you or your car.

*

She offers to help you choose a new outfit.
She's embarrassed by your clothes.

*

She suggests a girl's day out shopping.
She wants some new clothes.

Mother Nature is providential. She gives us
twelve years to develop a love for our children
before turning them into teenagers.
William Galvin, politician

Things You Should Never Say to a Teenager in Front of His/Her Friends

Don't you look cute in that?

✳

Make sure you're home by six o'clock.

✳

You look just like your dad/me.

✳

Do you want to dance?

✳

Bring your friends to the karaoke night.
I'm doing a duet with your dad.

✳

Who's my brave little soldier?

✳

I've got your favorite for dinner — Spaghetti Os!

✳

You used to have such a cute dimple on your bottom.

✳

You still can't sleep without your teddy, can you, sweetie?

✳

Give me a kiss.

Youthful Independence

Try to think back to when you were a teenager (horrible as it may be). From a teenage point of view, however cool your parents may be, they are way more embarrassing than anyone else's and will always say and do the wrong thing. And they can't possibly know what you're going through!

Remember, teenagers don't hate you, they hate the world and you're the nearest target!

The hardest thing for a mom to do is to let go. But teenagers need to assert some independence and occasionally (heaven forbid!) make their own mistakes. It's all part of the learning process.

The American Academy of Child and Adolescent Psychiatry (AACAP) suggest these golden rules for preparing yourselves, and your teenager, for this difficult period

✽

Provide a safe and loving home environment.

✽

Create an atmosphere of honesty, trust, and respect.

✽

Allow age-appropriate independence and assertiveness.

✽

Develop a relationship that encourages your teen
to talk to you when he/she is upset.

Teach responsibility for your teen's belongings and yours.

*

Teach basic responsibility for household chores.

*

Teach the importance of accepting limits.

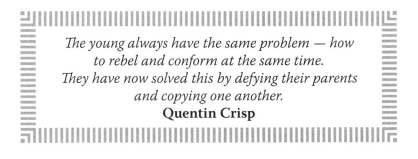

*The young always have the same problem — how
to rebel and conform at the same time.
They have now solved this by defying their parents
and copying one another.*
Quentin Crisp

Mom's Gone Shopping

Shopping is a pastime that universally divides the sexes. Women, on the whole, love it and men hate it. When a woman decides to go shopping there is one thing she absolutely shouldn't bring along — her children!

Unless the purpose of the shopping trip is to buy them clothes and shoes, or they are over the age of fourteen (and female, obviously), they are nothing but a hindrance and their presence will invariably lead to arguments, hair tearing, and, in the worst-case scenario, a very public nervous breakdown.

Tantrums in the aisles, sneaking things into baskets, and a constant chorus of "Mommy, can I *please* have this" is all you can expect if you drag them out, so wait until they are at school, at their grandparents', or at home with dad and ENJOY!

The Supermarket

Before having children you could hardly imagine that a trip to the grocery store could be a pleasurable experience. When you have tried it with three young ones, you realize the definition of stress-free shopping is a visit to the store *on your own*!

Follow these tips to make your trip down the aisles even more of a pleasure.

Tsk loudly at every badly behaved child in the store. You've seen your kids behave like that a million times, but the poor, beleaguered mother dragging her screaming two-year-old behind her while her four-year-old runs up and down the aisle with the shopping cart doesn't know that.

∗

Spend hours in the drugstore department, browse in the book section, and look at all the things you would usually whiz past if you were on a family shopping trip.

∗

Skip buying all the sweets and treats that the children asked you to bring back and, instead, stock up on exotic fruits they've never tried.

∗

Choose a supermarket with a clothes section. When you get home and moan that groceries are *so* expensive these days and that you've just spent $350, you don't have to mention the skirts, blouse, handbag, and beautiful leather boots that happened to have fallen into your shopping cart!

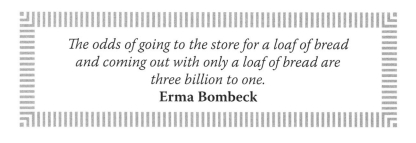

The odds of going to the store for a loaf of bread and coming out with only a loaf of bread are three billion to one.
Erma Bombeck

> *When women are depressed, they either eat*
> *or go shopping. Men invade another country.*
> *It's a whole different way of thinking.*
> **Elayne Boosler**

Clothes Shopping

For the ultimate shopping experience, take along a friend (or several) and make a day of it. You can arrange to go somewhere nice for lunch, and you'll have someone to ask "does my butt look big in this?" Again, it's no good taking the kids. If you try on a fantastic dress for that special occasion, howls of laughter and "Mommy, you look funny in that" will likely dampen your enthusiasm.

Have an idea what you are looking for. Read magazines or watch a fashion program before shopping. Otherwise, you may have "buyer's remorse."

✳

If you need a skirt, try not to come home with a pair of pants. As the busy supermom that you are, another relaxed shopping trip could be a long way off. If you intended to buy one thing, then bought another, it means you will still be longing for the original item as soon as the shopping trip is over.

✳

Try to avoid being diverted into children's departments or toy stores while you're on your shopping spree. Remember, that this is your time and you must put yourself first every once in a while. Take a note of anything you see for your kids and buy it another time — they'll understand!

✳

Have fun. If you are with friends, try on the most outrageous and inappropriate outfits you can find. The results can be hysterical.

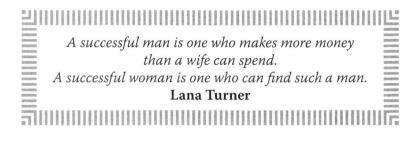

A successful man is one who makes more money than a wife can spend.
A successful woman is one who can find such a man.
Lana Turner

Shopping Purgatory

Even celebrities shop. Let's face it, they have the money. But it's not always a pleasant experience for them.

✳

On a trip to Rome, Sophia Loren decided to buy some bras. She hadn't accounted for the unwanted presence of a gabble of Italian men, and news soon spread like wildfire. A huge crowd soon gathered in and around the lingerie shop, trapping the actress in the dressing room. It took three fire brigades to break up the crowd.

✳

In 2003, heiress Paris Hilton arrived at Las Vegas airport with the fruits of her latest shopping trip in the city and couldn't understand why the flight attendants refused to let her board her plane to Los Angeles. It wasn't surprising when the purchases in dispute were a goat, a monkey, and ferret. "The flight attendants thought I was insane," recalled Paris. "They were like, 'This isn't a traveling circus — you're not bringing a goat on the plane!'" She managed to get her new pets home eventually, however, after treating them to a six-hour limo ride.

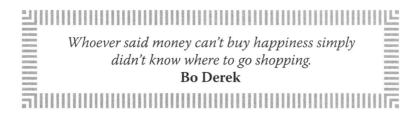

Whoever said money can't buy happiness simply didn't know where to go shopping.
Bo Derek

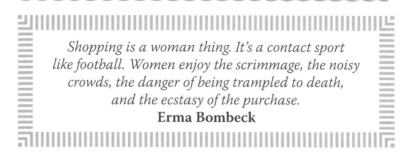

Shopping is a woman thing. It's a contact sport like football. Women enjoy the scrimmage, the noisy crowds, the danger of being trampled to death, and the ecstasy of the purchase.
Erma Bombeck

In 1989, at the age of fourteen, actress Drew Barrymore stole her mother's credit card, flew to Los Angeles, and went to a mall. Some time later, she was asked about her crazy trip. "What was the point of having a credit card," she replied, "if you weren't going to shop?"

✳

Rock star Courtney Love once spent so much money on her credit cards that when a BMW was fraudulently charged to her, she didn't even notice.

Shoppers in Paradise

Film director Mark Lewis was proud his mother came from the Bronx in New York. "She had a devilish sense of humor," he remarked. "She wanted her ashes spread through Bloomingdale's when she died. She said she'd bought a nice cashmere sweater there once. So my brother and I, we walked around the store spreading her ashes. It was like that scene when they spread the dirt from the tunnels around in *The Great Escape*."

✳

During an appearance on Bravo's *Inside the Actor's Studio* one evening, *Sex and the City* star Sarah Jessica Parker was asked what sound she loved the most. She answered without hesitation. "Ka-ching!"

Compulsive Shoppers

In 2002, actress Salma Hayek admitted that she had been having trouble battling an addiction. "It was a vice that got completely out of control," she confessed. It wasn't the usual Hollywood habit of drugs or alcohol, though. It was the Home Shopping Network

✳

Imelda Marcos, the high priestess of compulsive shoe shopping, once declared: "I have no weakness for shoes. I wear simple shoes — pumps. It is not one of my weaknesses." Later, when she fled the Philippines with her husband, she left 3,300 pairs of these "simple" shoes behind!

Actress Dolores Chaplin once remarked, "Any time I'm depressed, I buy high heels or underwear. That way, at the end of the year, I get a pretty good idea of my psychological state from my wardrobe!"

✳

In 2003, Angelina Jolie visited Macy's in Los Angeles. She chose some Ralph Lauren towels and then asked if she could try them out in the changing rooms. "I need to rub them against my body," she explained, "to see if they are soft enough." Let's hope she ended up buying them. . . .

Queen of Coupons

Susan J. Samtur has made a living out of saving money. Bringing up four sons in New York on a budget, Susan began to collect coupons to help with the weekly shopping. She became so good at this that, in 1973, she and husband, Steve, launched the magazine *Refundle Bundle*, which now has more than two million subscribers.

In 1978, a television reporter accompanied Susan to the supermarket, where she stacked her cart with $130 worth of groceries. When it came to paying for all her goods, Susan presented her coupons and paid the balance — all $7 of it! No doubt the cashier was delighted about having to process all those coupons.

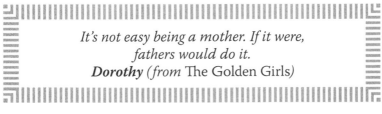

It's not easy being a mother. If it were,
fathers would do it.
Dorothy (*from* The Golden Girls)

Things You Wish
Your Mother Had Told You

Babies always wait until you have taken off their diaper to pee.

✻

Men never buy tasteful underwear.

✻

Most desserts are just as good if they're store-bought.
Remember: Stressed is desserts spelled backward.

✻

Lunching with your friends constitutes child care, as long as
they have children, too.

✻

It always rains at school pickup time.

If men man the barbecue, they must receive ALL the praise — even if you've spent all morning in the kitchen preparing the side dishes.

✳

You can't argue with a five-year-old without sounding like one yourself.

✳

When a baby is awake, you want him/her to be asleep, and when he/she is asleep you want him/her awake. Conversely, when a teenager is at home, you want him/her to go out. When he/she is out, you want him/her back in the house.

✳

Life's too short to bake a cake.

✳

If you have children of your own, you will inevitably end up sounding just like your mother!

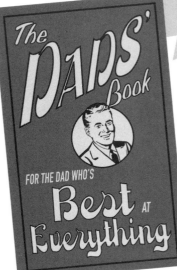